HIGH PRAISE 2

A SECOND BOOK OF ANTHEMS
FOR UPPER-VOICE CHOIRS

Selected & edited by Barry Rose.

NOVELLO
London

NOV020680

FRONT COVER Edward Reginald Frampton, *A Carol*, Bridgeman Art Library
BACK COVER photograph of Barry Rose by Timothy Hands

COVER DESIGN Sue Clarke

MUSIC SETTING Stave Origination

NOV020680
ISBN 1-84449-370-9

HEAD OFFICE
14/15 Berners Street,
London W1T 3LJ
England
Tel +44 (0)20 7434 0066
Fax +44 (0)20 7287 6329

SALES AND HIRE
Music Sales Limited,
Newmarket Road,
Bury St Edmunds,
Suffolk IP33 3YB
England
Tel +44 (0)1284 702600
Fax +44 (0)1284 768301

www.chesternovello.com
e-mail: music@musicsales.co.uk

Other anthologies by Barry Rose available from Novello:

High Praise NOV032118
Merrily on High NOV032121
More than Hymns 1 NOV040043
More than Hymns 2 NOV040044
More than Psalms NOV040062
Sing Low NOV381000

Contents

Notes on the music

Ave Maria · Matthew Martin
Written for a wedding in 1997, whilst he was Organ Scholar at Magdalen College, Oxford, Matthew Martin's anthem was originally scored for solo soprano and solo tenor. He has now re-arranged it for two sopranos for inclusion in *High Praise 2*. The delicate and flowing vocal lines call for legato singing throughout, and the descant that begins in bar 33 could well be sung by a soloist or semi-chorus. The accompaniment is suitable for piano or organ. Latin is a grateful language in which to sing, and the style of Italianate pronunciation we generally use calls for long vowels – e.g. a = ah, i = ee, u = oo. These will help your singers achieve a legato line.

Ave verum · W. A. Mozart, arr. Brian Trant
Amongst the best-known of all choral pieces, Mozart manages to say more in just forty-six bars of *Ave verum corpus* than some composers are able to say in as many pages! It was written at the beginning of June 1791, six months before he died. Dedicated to his friend Anton Stoll, choirmaster at the parish church in Baden, near Vienna, it was first performed a few days later on the feast of Corpus Christi (8 June). The text dates from the fourteenth century and is in honour of the Blessed Sacrament. In the four lines used by Mozart, it describes Christ's Incarnation, his Passion and Suffering on the Cross.

Usually sung in the key of D major, the arrangement here is a minor third higher to allow three-part upper-voice singing. Apart from 'sotto voce', Mozart did not put any instructions in his score, but if you follow the arranger's suggested dynamic markings, both the words and music will have a natural rise and fall. This piece is not without its challenges in pitch, and great care should be taken with the descending chromatic intervals, and especially in the tuning of the alto part between bars 22 and 29.

The bringer of life · Andrew Jackman
Residents of the county of Norfolk in England, Diane Jackman and her late husband Andrew collaborated on *The Bringer of Life* in 1987, and it was first sung at a Christmas festival that year in St. Andrew's Church, Norwich. The words present the message of Christmas in a way that seems highly relevant to the start of the twenty-first century, and in concert or service, it might be appropriate to have them read aloud before your choir sings them.

Brought up as a church chorister in north west London, Andrew Jackman showed a natural flair as arranger and composer across a wide musical spectrum. His music here is individual, lovingly crafted, and shows a rare understanding of text painting. The start of verse 4 ('Mary') could present

problems of word emphasis, and you will need to be sure that your singers stress the first, rather than the second syllable, with its longer sustained note.

A Christmas Carol · Arnold Bax
This work is one of a cycle of *Seven songs for high voice and piano* originally written for solo soprano, and composed in 1919. Arnold Bax was also an accomplished pianist, and the accompaniment here bears all the hallmarks of someone who understands and uses the tonal colours and wide range of the piano keyboard – organists may need to make some slight adjustments.

The well known macaronic text comes from a mid fifteenth-century manuscript in the library of Trinity College, Cambridge, though the composer has taken certain liberties by using the phrase 'res miranda' (from verse 2) in the first verse, and repeating 'Alleluia' after each verse. The music carries an air of mystery and other-worldliness and benefits from touches of musical rubato. It also makes considerable demands on the singer's breath control in such places as the start of verse 2 and verse 3. Choirs can stagger the breathing at these points but a soloist will have to work extremely hard to convey the meaning of the words at these places.

Come, my way, my truth, my life! · William H. Harris
Here is an adaptation for upper voices of an earlier anthem setting for SATB choir, and it dates from the time that the composer, formerly organist of St. George's Chapel, Windsor, was living in retirement, in Petersfield, Hampshire.

The key of D flat major was a favourite of William Harris, and its richness lends a special grandeur to George Herbert's well loved text. This is one of those pieces where you need to persuade your singers to think of fewer beats in the bar than are indicated by the time-signature – i.e. two in a bar rather than four, or even three. That way the music will flow, and just the key words will be given the correct emphasis. It is also important that you conduct the piece in this way, since indicating four beats in a bar will instil lumpy singing in your choir. May I make a plea for the observance of the printed dynamics? These are carefully marked, and will bring light and shade into singing, as well as understanding to your listeners.

God be in my head · H. Walford Davies
The text comes from a Book of Hours of 1514, and was first published as a hymn in the *Oxford Hymn Book* (1908). At that time, Walford Davies was organist and choirmaster at London's Temple Church, and it is quite possible that he wrote his now well-

known anthem for his own choir to sing as a short introit, usually sung from the round church (at the west end of the building) at the beginning of each Sunday morning service. This arrangement comes from a 1940s collection for upper voices. The first two bars, marked here as solo, could well be played as an organ/piano introduction. With a choir that has some low altos, the penultimate note of the last bar could be split into two crotchet Fs (the second an octave lower than the first), rather than the sustained higher minim F given here.

God be with you till we meet again · Barry Rose
It is appropriate that this anthem-style setting of hymn words was written for an American choir, since the text also originates from there. The author, Jeremiah Eames Rankin, was minister at the First Congregational Church in Washington DC, when, in 1882, he wrote the hymn as a way of explaining the true meaning of 'goodbye' – a shortened form of 'God be with you'.

My setting was written for the boys and girls' choirs at Grace Church, Lower Broadway, New York, and since one of the choristers was an able flautist, I was asked to add a flute part, which can also be played on the organ.

A grateful heart · Mary Plumstead
Here is a well-known and deservedly popular piece, specially written for the wedding of Angela and Brian Rayner Cook. As a solo baritone, Brian had previously sung some of Mary Plumstead's songs, and it was his suggestion that she should set George Herbert's text for their marriage service.

Very much a self-taught composer, Mary Plumstead later became a lecturer in composition, and advocated what she described as 'self composition'. Her music here is both affectionate and tuneful, as well as being an example of effective word setting.

The original text did not repeat 'Thou that hast given so much to me', but by doing so at the end, with a variation of the opening phrase, a complete musical unity is achieved.

Here I am, Lord · Daniel Schutte, arr. Andrew Parnell
One of the most popular modern hymn-songs of recent years, with its memorable melody, and a text based on Isaiah, Chapter 6. Both the words and music are by Daniel Schutte SJ, and were written in the 1970s, whilst he was a student at the Jesuit Seminary in St. Louis, Missouri. Now living in San Francisco, he continues to write music for parish worship, and also lectures on music in liturgy.

Andrew Parnell has written this extended arrangement for *High Praise 2*. Its roots were in a shorter and simpler version he made in the mid 1990s for the choristers of St. Albans Abbey. The rhythmic accompaniment immediately creates the mood for

the singers, and is suited to either organ or piano. The ingenious juxtaposition of the opening melody against the refrain in verse 2 (bars 38 to 51) will need careful balancing and observance of the printed dynamics. Great care should also be taken to see that the descant does not dominate the melody (bar 55 onwards). Again the dynamic markings are clear and need to be observed to achieve the correct effects.

Here, O my Lord · Barry Rose
(An SATB version is included in *More than Hymns 2*, NOV040044)
The words are taken from Communion hymn, written in 1855 by Dr. Horatius Bonar, a Free Church minister in Kelso, Scotland. The original had ten verses, but the three set here are the ones found in most hymnals.

The music was written in 1998 for the boys and girls of St. Paul's Episcopal Church choir, Fairfield, Connecticut, as they were about to set out on a visit to England, and they first sang it in Ely Cathedral as a Communion motet. The music is quite easy to learn, and perhaps the real challenge is in singing the words clearly and with understanding. The elision of 'here' to 'O' will make it sound like 'hero' to your listeners, and the same problems could prevail in bars 6-7 ('and handle') and bar 10 ('and all'). So please take the time and trouble to work on the text – the effort will be well worthwhile.

Hills of the North · Herbert Howells
A veritable *tour-de-force* for upper-voice choirs, this extended and exciting setting was composed in 1977 when it was given its first performance in Bristol Cathedral, at the Clifton High School for Girls Centenary 'Rose Day' Service. Herbert Howells, who was in the congregation on that day, later wrote about the singing of the school's 68-strong Centenary Choir, 'they sang it as if they loved it'. The manuscript was later given to the choir's director, Sheila Forster, and in 2000 it was first published by Bristol Cathedral Enterprises.

The text is by the Rev. Charles Oakley, and was written between 1856 and 1863, whilst he was Rector of Wickwar in Gloucestershire. Usually associated with Advent or Epiphany, it is really a missionary hymn, with separate verses based on all four compass points, and neatly brought together in the last verse. From the opening two-bar introduction, the music is unmistakeably Howells, and the voices make an immediate dramatic impact with their ringing 'Hills of the North'. Musical subtleties abound, and everywhere the text is aptly painted, often making considerable demands on both the confidence and technique of the singers. To help the interpretation, Howells wrote that in performance the singers should think of the minim (half note) as being the actual beat, and not the crotchet (quarter note). As far as initial learning, I would suggest that this is one piece where the parts could be learned separately, and put together later. It is a piece which would suit a larger than usual choir, and has been performed to great effect by massed voices at two celebratory gatherings of girls choirs from English cathedrals.

How like an angel came I down · Malcolm Archer

An eloquent and memorable setting of the first three verses of Thomas Traherne's poem, *Wonder*. Although he lived in the seventeenth century, the majority of Traherne's poetry remained unknown until 1896, when by chance, two of his manuscripts were discovered on a bookstall in London. There was also a later discovery in 1908 of a further manuscript in the British Museum. The eight-verse poem is typical of the metaphysical poets, with its elaborate imagery relating to the works of God.

The music dates from 2000, and was first sung at a Choral Evensong in Salisbury Cathedral during August that year. It was commissioned by the Music Masters' and Mistresses' Association in memory of the late Stanley Milnes, long-serving Director of Music at Edge Grove Preparatory School, Hertfordshire. Malcolm Archer achieves a real sense of tenderness and beauty in his eloquently written phrases, and the various key changes are seamless and expertly highlight the text. I was privileged to conduct the first performance and the perfect match of words and music had a profound effect on me, as I'm sure it will on all who sing it.

How lovely are Thy dwellings fair · Eric Thiman

Some verses from a metrical version of Psalm 84, written in 1648 by John Milton, one of *Nine of the Psalmes done in Metre*. Eric Thiman's music was written nearly three hundred years later, and is a typical example of the composer's musical craftsmanship and sense of melodic flow. Milton's words would originally have been sung to a hymn tune, beginning on an up beat, sometimes throwing the emphasis on to what should be unemphasised syllables. Here, in this setting, the start of verse 2 ('happy who in Thy house reside') receives a more sympathetic and aware treatment. The whole effect is one of assured tranquillity, with some striking modulations which demand more dramatic singing. As with many of the pieces in this collection, the composer has been punctilious in his dynamic and other musical markings, and observance of these will help bring the text to life, both for the singers and listeners.

A Hymn to the Virgin · Robert Spearing

The text, which has been set by many composers, dates from c. 1450, and is taken from the Sloane manuscript 2593.

Robert Spearing's setting was written in 1971 when he was completing his studies at the Royal College of Music in London, where he was a composition student of Herbert Howells. It was commissioned by the choirmaster of St. Barnabas' Church, Purley, Surrey, UK, to celebrate the 10th anniversary of the choir he had founded at the church, and the trumpet part was played by a pupil from a local school. The instrumental introduction needs to be played and sung without any sense of metronomic beat ('senza misura') though a gently flowing rhythm is established when the voices enter (bar 3). From then on, the music builds towards its climax at the alleluias, though you should note the composer's instruction to sing these sweetly (bar 13). The opening verse could be sung by a soloist or semi-chorus, and the learning process for the remaining verses can easily be shortened by both parts learning their phrases in unison, noting that some of the end notes differ.

I sing of a maiden · Bryan Hesford

Bryan Hesford wrote his setting in the early 1960s, whilst he was organist of Wymondham Abbey, Norfolk, and dedicated it to the composer Arthur Milner (1894-1972).

The instructions at the start give every clue needed to the vocal and musical approach you should take, and the gentle and lilting folk-like melody is a perfect companion to the words. In bars 24-40 it might be advisable to reduce the number of voices on the upper part, so that the melody continues to have the prominence it deserves.

Lift thine eyes · Felix Mendelssohn

Originally written as a duet, you may be surprised to learn that the popular three-part version of *Lift thine eyes* was born amongst grimy heaps of coal and coke lining a canal bank! It was in the heart of the city of Birmingham, England on 26 August, 1846, and Mendelssohn had just conducted the first performance of *Elijah* in the Town Hall. He took some friends for a post-concert stroll by the canal, and it was there that he announced the changes he felt he now needed to make to his new oratorio, one of which was re-writing *Lift thine eyes* as a trio. In the oratorio, the exhausted Elijah now sleeps in the wilderness, and the previous recitative tells us the 'the angels of the Lord encamp around all them that fear him'. I suggest that the key words for your singing should be angelic and legato, with some elegant long phrases, rather than a pronounced break at each comma.

The Lord is my Shepherd · Franz Schubert

Perhaps the best-loved of all the psalm texts, Franz Schubert wrote his setting of Psalm 23 in December, 1820, under the title *Gott ist mein Hirt*. It was dedicated to Anna Froelich, a friend who taught singing at the Vienna Conservatoire, and who was looking for an examination piece for some of her students. Originally in four parts, it is included here as a duet, with both the original German, and an English translation which remains as faithful as possible to Schubert's original musical notation. The pastoral mood of the words is immediately apparent in the triplets of the accompaniment, whilst the singers weave their melodic legato lines in duple time. The key words for the singers are elegant and sustained phrases throughout, with a suitable change of mood and sound for the more dramatic 'Yea, though I walk through death's dark vale'.

Magnificat and Nunc Dimittis "Washington" · David Hogan

An accomplished singer, pianist, organist and vocal coach, David Hogan was invited to compose an SATB setting of the Magnificat and Nunc Dimittis in celebration of the completion and consecration of the National Cathedral in Washington, DC, in 1989. In 1994, he wrote this setting for upper voices, dedicating it to the cathedral choristers.

The exultant mood of the Magnificat is immediately captured by the infectiously rhythmic organ part which reappears in various places, and the choral parts pick up on that mood, are memorable, and bear all the hallmarks of having been written by someone who understands the voice. The opening of the Nunc Dimittis has a haunting and timeless quality with its minor key, but this soon gives way to the assurance of the text, culminating in a return to the joyfully rhythmic Gloria used in the Magnificat.

Choirs of all abilities can tackle this piece. The key words are *perfect rhythm* both for singers and accompanist, and perhaps this is an occasion when you might check the composer's metronome markings, to see what tempo he had in mind. David Hogan lost his life when a TWA Boeing 747 en route to Paris, blew up and disintegrated over Long Island Sound in July, 1996.

A New Year Carol · Robert Ruutel

Born and educated in Bristol, Robert Ruutel was a bass Choral Scholar at Exeter Cathedral and later a vicar-choral with Wells Cathedral choir. A *New Year Carol* was written for a former chorister at Wells and received its first performance there at an evensong in January 2002, when it was sung by the cathedral's girls choir. Originally conceived as a duet, the music provides an original and relatively simple setting for upper voices whilst conveying a sense of optimism for the new year, mingled with awe at the majesty of the elevation of the Host at the Eucharist. 'Levy dew' is assumed to be a corruption of the French 'lever à dieu', or 'lift to the Lord'. The origin of the text is unknown. In 1932 it was included in a collection of poems edited by Walter de la Mare, a former chorister of St. Paul's Cathedral, and since then there has been much speculation as to the meaning of the symbolism it portrays. It seems to relate to the church, with its allusions to the East and the West Door, whilst the Fair Maid could well be a gilded statue of the Blessed Virgin Mary.

This setting can be performed with a solo voice leading the full choir, or by two equal choirs, but in either case, the final bars should *always* be sung by a solo voice, and with absolutely no trace of vibrato.

Notre Père · John Tavener

A setting of the Lord's Prayer, composed to the French text, following a commission from Les Petits Chanteurs de Saint-André, based in the Alsatian town of Colmar. It was this choir which gave the first performance in Bayswater, London, on 1 June, 1997 on the occasion of the baptism of Tavener's daughter, Sofia, at the house of the Archbishop Gregorios of Thyateira and Great Britain.

With its major and minor triads in similar motion, and some repeated themes, learning should not be very difficult, though the first trebles/sopranos will need to take care with the tuning of their B naturals and B flats in bars 7, 8 and 9. Some choirs tend to fight shy of singing French, and for those not used to that language, it might be helpful to bring in a French speaker as a coach, and for the singers to say the words in rhythm before they actually sing the notes. The instruction in bars 5 and 6, regarding Byzantine chant, may be confusing, but the clue is in the word 'microtone' – i.e. less than a semitone. So at that point a small 'catch' in the voice from the upper side of the following note should achieve the desired effect. Perhaps choir directors will demonstrate!

Nunc Dimittis · Geoffrey Burgon

Originally written for television, Geoffrey Burgon's setting of the Nunc Dimittis has become firmly established in the repertoire for upper-voice choirs, both in concert, and also in the liturgy. It was in 1979 that he wrote the incidental music for the BBC serialisation of John Le Carré's *Tinker, Tailor, Soldier, Spy*, and whilst most of his music was scored for string quartet, he added the organ and a haunting trumpet obligato to the Nunc Dimittis, sung by a solo treble (Paul Phoenix) as the closing credits were set against a shot of the Radcliffe Camera in Oxford. The elegant and sustained phrases suit both solo and massed singing, whilst the setting of the Gloria achieves a rare delicacy with its hushed ending. The trumpet part can readily be played on the organ. The composer later added a two-part setting of the Magnificat (CH55253), commissioned by the Royal Choral Society.

Panis angelicus · César Franck, arr. Henry Geehl

The text is the sixth verse of the hymn 'Sacris solemniis juncta sint gaudia', written around 1264, by Thomas Aquinas at the request of Pope Urban IV when he established the feast of Corpus Christi. Just over six hundred years later, in 1872, César Franck, the organist of the church of Ste. Clotilde in Paris, wrote the now famous melody, originally scored for tenor, organ, harp, cello and double bass. Since then it has been arranged for many combinations, both instrumental and vocal, and this arrangement, for three-part choir, dates from 1951, a time when choirs such as the Luton Girls' Choir were enjoying great popularity in concerts, recordings and broadcasts.

Pie Jesu · Andrew Lloyd Webber

Probably the best-known movement of Andrew Lloyd Webber's Requiem, premiered in St. Thomas's Church, New York, on 25 February 1985. The work had previously been recorded by Winchester Cathedral choir, and they also took part in the New York performance, together with the same soloists. The duet in *Pie Jesu* was sung by Sarah Brightman (soprano), and Paul Miles-Kingston (treble), and their award-winning recording was the only 'single' ever issued by the classical division of HMV records. In this arrangement, we have transposed some of the chorus parts, (e.g. bars 29 and 30), but otherwise the piece remains unaltered. If possible, solo 1 should be a soprano, and solo 2 a treble, as the composer originally intended.

Praise · George Dyson

The second of *Three Songs of Praise*, this setting of George Herbert's poem 'Let all the world' dates from 1919, whilst the composer was teaching at Winchester College, and was probably written for the college's treble-voice quiristers to sing in chapel. It was later arranged for four-part choir – see *More than Hymns 1* (NOV040043).

Dyson's music is immediately joyful and grand, and paints the text so as to underline the last line of the poem, both verses using the repeated words 'My God'.

Some performers (and listeners) may be startled by the sudden key change in bar 21, and it is here that the accompanist could use a touch of rubato to savour the moment. This is one of those pieces where you may have to ask your choir to overplay their endings to the words – especially at 'sing' and 'king' which, with the loud accompaniment at those points could well end up sounding like 'sin' and 'kin' at those points – NOT what your listeners want to hear! (The sung *ng* is always a useful vocal exercise for choir trainers, particularly to help the forward placement of the voice. Try a scale on consecutive *ng-ah* sounds).

A prayer · Richard Lloyd

A former organist of Hereford and Durham Cathedrals, Richard Lloyd is also known as a composer of choral and organ music. This setting of Irene Cavenaugh's text dates from his time at Hereford, and is dedicated to his wife, Morwenna. The graceful melodic lines appear to be quite easy, but the whole effect of the words and music can only be achieved by building the dynamics from an *mp* start to the *forte* climax from bar 43 onwards, and then have a controlled and *piano* ending – not as easy as it seems. There are also some challenges to be overcome in diction – e.g. take care not to elide 'this' to 'all' (bars 12 and 30) and 'thee' to 'adore' (bars 20 and 38) –

and you will also need to take care to observe the commas in bars 50, 51 and 52.

Prayer of St. Francis of Assisi · Arthur Bliss

Although the words are ascribed to St. Francis of Assisi, this is only through an association with an image of the Saint on a prayer card with these words printed on the reverse side. First published in a French magazine, *La Clochette*, in 1912, the author remains unknown. It was translated into the well known English version in 1936.

Several years later, in the 1950s and 60s, the Orpington Junior Singers were regularly heard in concert halls and on the radio. Founded in 1949, their conductor was Sheila Mossman, whose life was tragically cut short in 1971 at the age of 48, and it was to her memory that the choir's president, Sir Arthur Bliss, then Master of the Queen's Musick, wrote his setting of *Lord, make me an instrument of thy peace.*

With its four unaccompanied parts over which there is a short solo, the music deftly paints the words, and nowhere more so than the opposites in each line (i.e. 'hatred' and 'love', 'sadness' and 'joy', etc). The writing reflects the great accomplishment of Sheila Mossman's choir, and today's choirs will need to spend time working hard on tuning and ensemble to give them the confidence to sing this inspirational setting. They will be more than amply rewarded for their efforts.

The Preces and Responses · John Abdenour

Currently organist and choirmaster at St. Paul's Episcopal Church, Fairfield, Connecticut, John Abdenour wrote his setting of the Preces and Responses in 2002. The music is through-composed, the tempo is established at the beginning of each bar in which the choir begins to sing, and the composer suggests that the Priest's/Cantor's part may be sung at the choir's pitch. Having performed this setting with the massed forces of three choirs, I can recommend its originality and effectiveness, even if a glance at the key signature and initial accompaniments may deter some faint-hearted organists! We found that bars 19 to 32 needed the most careful choral rehearsal for accurate rhythm, as did bars 14 to 16 for pitch. The music is memorable, well matched to the words, and is something your choir will enjoy the challenge of learning.

Psalm 150 · Barry Rose

Amongst the best-known of the psalms, 'O praise God in his holiness' has been set by many composers, and when I was invited to write yet another setting, it was not just for the choirs and the occasion – a children's choir festival in New York – but also to provide a piece they could take back and sing in their own parishes. In several places the second treble part can be omitted, and for those choirs who cannot manage three parts, the nine notes for the thirds can easily be omitted. The music has one objective – to paint the text, both in the vocal and piano/organ parts, and the key words for your singing should be carefree and joyful. You'll find it will sound that way if you actually look the part! (For those choirs which sing 'Spirit' instead of 'Ghost' in bar 46, it is possible to insert two quavers, but impossible then to take a breath at that point.)

Through the day · Alan Ridout

This contemplative anthem for evensong is the direct result of a telephone conversation between the composer and me. I was lamenting the lack of suitable upper-voice anthems based on words of evening hymns, when Alan Ridout generously offered to write a piece specially for us at St. Albans. 'You choose the text', he said, and true to his word, the finished work arrived a week later.

The author is Thomas Kelly, ordained into the Irish Episcopal Church in 1792 from which he later seceded and founded a sect of his own. He wrote 751 hymns and this particular text has appeared in several books, often sung to a chorale-style melody by C.H. Dretzel (1698-1775). Alan Ridout's gently flowing music is beautifully matched to the text, and sometimes makes effective use of the doubling of the melody an octave lower. Here, as in the descant, you will need to select your singers according to their comfortable range, and we found that just three or four well chosen voices were suitable for the descant 'Ah' phrases in the second verse, as well as the high ending. It is also worth checking your speed against the composer's metronome marking – that is the ideal tempo at which to aim.

The virgin's slumber-song · Max Reger

A prolific composer throughout his comparatively short life, Max Reger is probably best remembered for his colourful and chromatic organ music. In this cradle song, originally entitled *Maria Wiegenlied*, he uses a much more simple and direct style, which might well have been inspired by a popular German Christmas song *Joseph lieber Joseph mein*. Reger's music is in the same style, and bars 23-26 have the identical opening phrase. As a Catholic (though excommunicated), Reger may have been drawn to the Marian theme of Martin Boelitz's poem and he scored the song for solo soprano and piano. This two-part arrangement dates from soon after the composer's death, and has an English version of the text by Edward Teschemacher, well known at that time as the lyricist of such popular songs as *I'll walk beside you* and *No rose in all the world*. Delicacy is the key word for the singers, with that lilting quality depicting a mother gently rocking her baby's cradle.

Who can express the noble acts of the Lord? · Samuel Sebastian Wesley

Here is the central section of the large-scale anthem *O give thanks unto the Lord*, one of the most demanding unison arias your choir can tackle, with a huge range – just one note short of two octaves! Organist of Leeds Parish Church, and at four cathedrals (Hereford, Exeter, Winchester and Gloucester), Samuel Sebastian Wesley wrote many fine anthems and settings, though this splendid piece, based on Psalm 106, is not amongst the best known.

Who can express? was originally conceived for a solo treble, but sounds equally well with massed voices. That can also solve problems over the length of the phrases, by the use of staggered breathing. The metronome marking indicates that the piece needs to keep moving, and it will help if the singers think in minims (half notes) rather than crotchets (quarter notes). In the original, the choir trebles lead into the start of the aria. Since we don't have that lead, we have added a four bar introduction.

Barry Rose

Ave Maria

The Angelic Salutation

Matthew Martin (b. 1976)

fru - ctus ven - tris tu - i Je - sus.

San - cta Ma - ri - a, Ma - ter De - i,

San - cta Ma - ri - a, Ma - ter De - i, Ma - ter

Ma - ter De - - i, o - ra pro no - bis

De - - i, o - ra pro no - bis pec - ca -

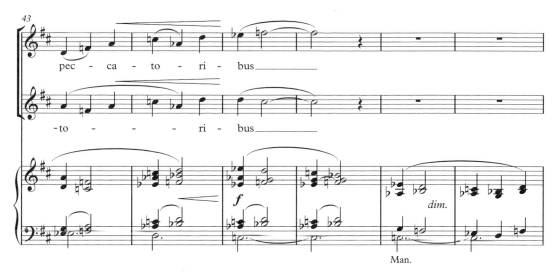

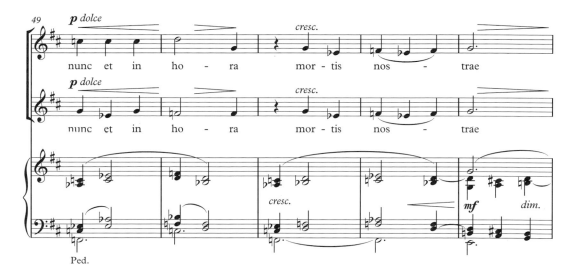

for the Girls' Choir of the
Mellow Lane Comprehensive Secondary School, Hayes

Ave verum

14th century Eucharistic hymn

W.A. Mozart (1756-91)
arr. Brian Trant (1910-95)

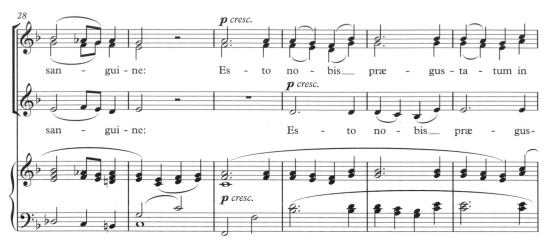

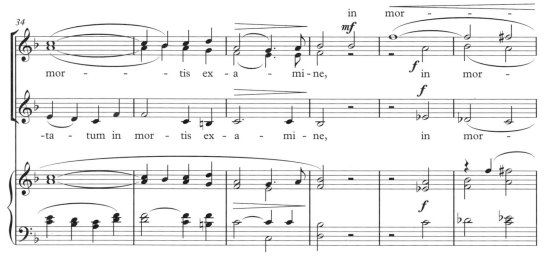

Hail, true Body, born of Mary the Virgin, truly suffered and immolated,
on the cross for mankind. Whose side was pierced, and it flowed with
water and blood. Let it be for us a pretaste before our weighing and
judgement at death.

The bringer of life

Diane Jackman (b. 1946)　　　　　　　　　　　　Andrew Jackman (1946-2003)

8

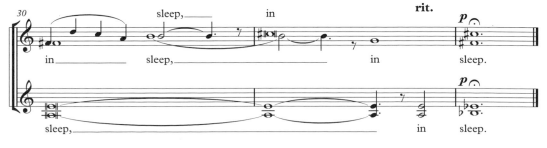

* There should be a longer break between the end of verse 3 and the beginning of verse 4.

to my sister, Evelyn

A Christmas Carol

15th century

Arnold Bax (1883-1953)

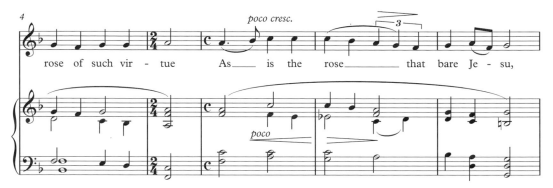

Orchestral accompaniment available on hire.

© Copyright 1919 by J. & W. Chester, London.

rose con - tain - ed was Heaven____ and earth____ in

lit - tle____ space, Res mi - ran - da, res____ mi -

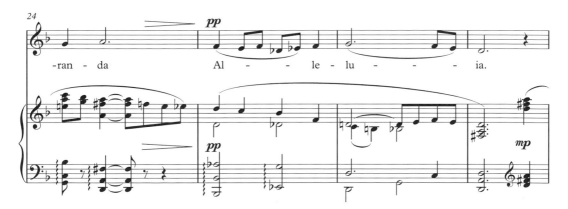

-ran - da Al - le - lu - ia.

By this

rose_ we_may well see There be one God in_ Per - sons three,_____

_____ Pa - res for - ma, Al - le - lu - ia,

al - le - lu - ia.

The an - gels sung-en the shep-herds un -

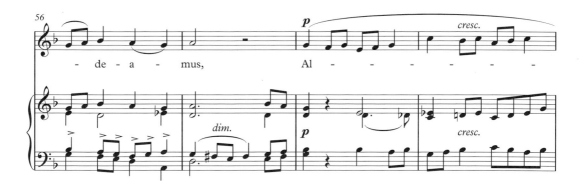

mirth, And_ fol - - low_ we this_ joy - ous_ birth,_

Tran - se - a - mus Al - - le - lu - - ia.

-ia.

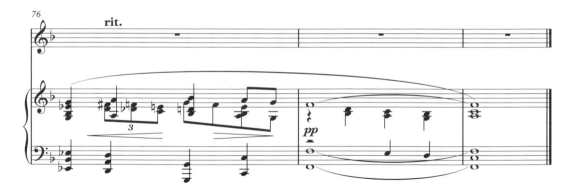

Come, my way, my truth, my life!

George Herbert (1593-1633)   William H. Harris (1883-1973)

Also published for SATB and Organ (NOV281224)

death, such a life_____ as kill-eth death.

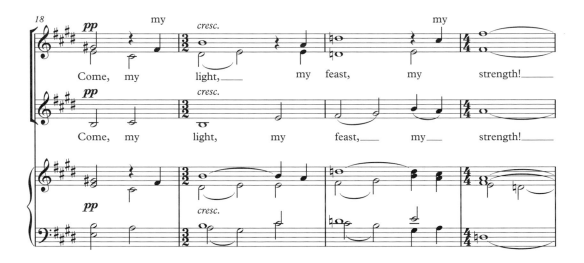

Come, my light,_____ my feast, my_____ strength!_____

Come, my light,_____ my feast,_____ my_____ strength!_____

_____ Such a light as shows a feast, such a feast as mends in

_____ Such a light,_____ such a feast as mends in

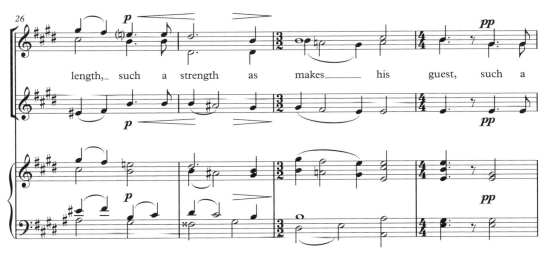

length,＿ such a strength as makes＿＿ his guest, such a

strength as makes his guest. Come, my

joy,＿＿ my love,＿ my heart!＿＿＿＿＿＿ Such a

joy as none can move, such a love as none can part,__ such a

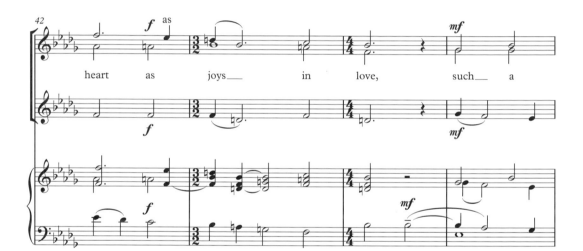

heart as joys__ in love, such__ a

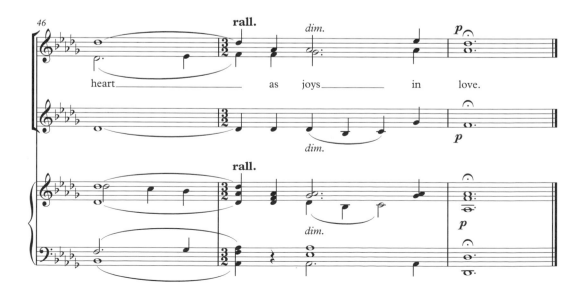

heart_____ as joys_____ in love.

God be in my head

Words from an old Sarum primer (1558)   H. Walford Davies (1869-1941)

for the girl and boy choristers of Grace Church, New York, U.S.A.

God be with you till we meet again

Jeremiah Eames Rankin (1828-1904)

Barry Rose (b. 1934)

† play only if no flute

* or a few voices

with____ you, till we meet____ a - gain.

God be with you till we meet____ a - gain, 'Neath his

Ped. (organ)

col 8ve ad lib. (al fine) (piano)

wings pro-tect - ing hide you, dai - ly man-na still pro - vide you: God be

* a few voices

* 3 equal parts

for Angela and Brian Rayner Cook

A grateful heart

George Herbert (1593-1633)   Mary Plumstead (1905-80)

me, As if Thy bless - ings had spare

days: But such a heart, whose pulse may be Thy

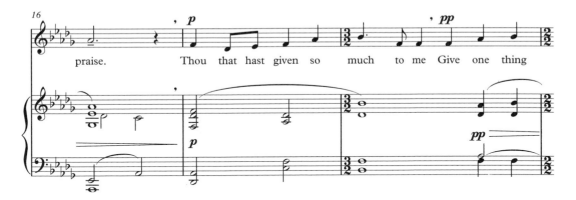

praise. Thou that hast given so much to me Give one thing

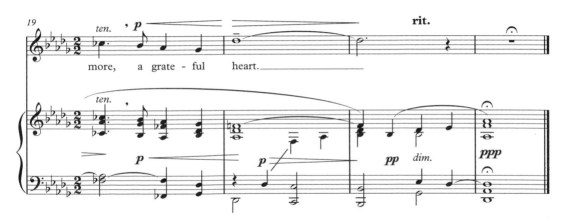

more, a grate - ful heart.

Here I am, Lord

Daniel Schutte
(based on Isaiah 6)

Daniel Schutte, S.J. (b. 1947)
arr. Andrew Parnell (b. 1954)

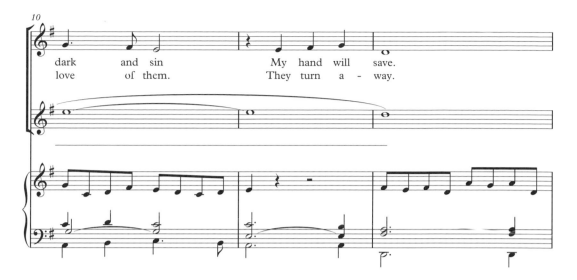

31 (1.)
go, Lord,_____ if You lead me._____

34 (1.)
_____ I will hold Your peo - ple in my heart.

38 2.
am, Lord._____ Is it I, Lord?_____

pp *sotto voce e leggiero*
I, the Lord of snow and rain, I have borne my

f

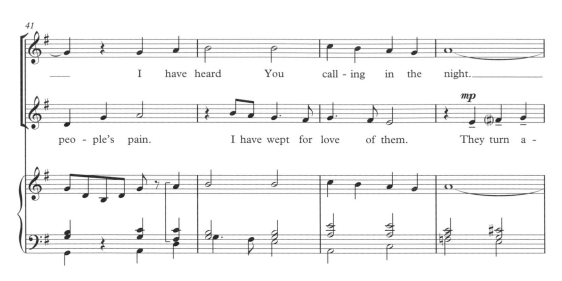

I have heard You call-ing in the night.

peo-ple's pain. I have wept for love of them. They turn a-

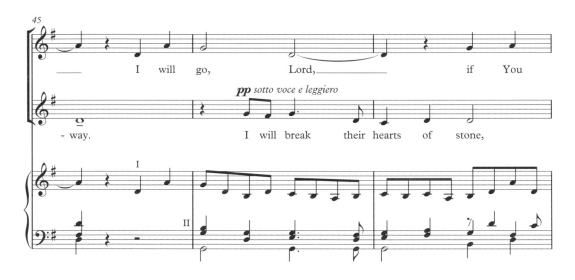

I will go, Lord, if You

-way. I will break their hearts of stone,

pp *sotto voce e leggiero*

lead me. I will hold Your

Give them hearts for love a-lone. I will speak my

* 2 equal parts from here

for Vincent Edwards and the Choristers of Saint Paul's Church, Fairfield, USA

Here, O my Lord

Horatius Bonar (1808-89)　　　　　　　　　　　　　　Barry Rose (b. 1934)

hand th' e-ter-nal grace, And all my wear-i-ness up - on thee lean.

Here would I

feed up - on the bread of God, Here drink with

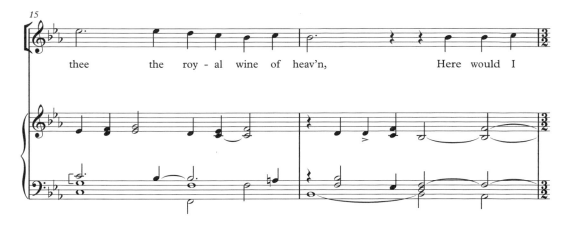

thee the roy - al wine of heav'n, Here would I

lay a - side each earth - ly load, Here taste a - fresh the calm of sin for -

- giv'n.

A FEW VOICES *mp*

ah _____

- giv'n.

f

I have no help but

* the tune (lower part) must be prominent here, but the final triad should be equally balanced.

to Sheila Forster and the Centenary Choir
[of Clifton High School for Girls]

Hills of the North

Charles Edward Oakley (1832-65) Herbert Howells (1892-1983)

The music for *Hills of the North* is printed by permission of Bristol Cathedral Enterprises Ltd, owners of the music copyright.

Though ab-sent long, your Lord___ is___ nigh; He___

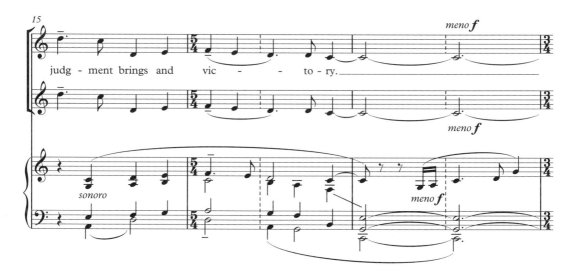

judg-ment brings and vic - - to-ry.___

a little less fast (♩ = c. 100)

Isles of the South-ern seas,___

Man.

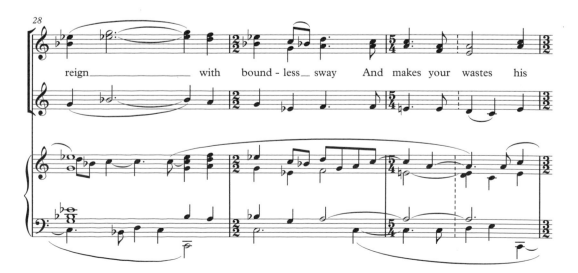

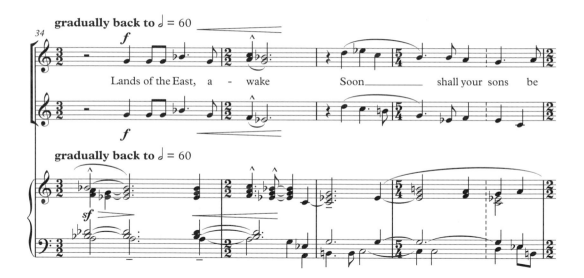

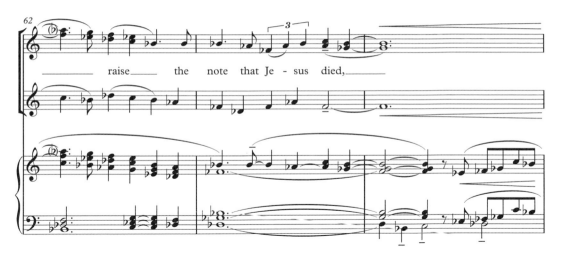

22
mf
Deep in your cor - al caves Pent be each war - ring breeze;
mf
mp
Ped.
(tutti)
25
p
Lulled be your rest - less waves;
f
cresc.
He comes to
mf
f
cresc.
28
reign with bound - less sway And makes your wastes his

raise the note that Je-sus died,

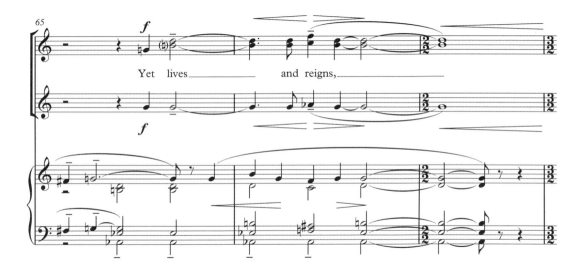

Yet lives and reigns,

Je - sus, Je - sus died, yet lives and reigns; the

allarg.

Cru - ci - fied._____

cresc. molto

a tempo primo, quasi

ff

Shout while ye jour - ney home;_____

a tempo primo, quasi

ff

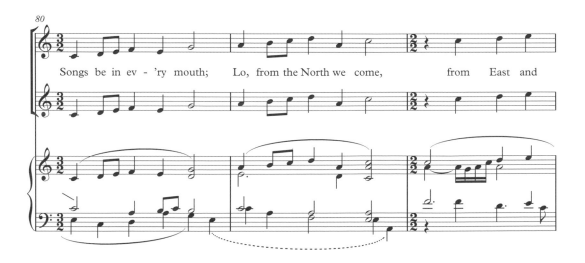

Songs be in ev - 'ry mouth; Lo, from the North we come, from East and

West_____ and South;_____ Ci - ty of God, the

bond_____ are___ free;_____ We___ come to live and

allarg.

reign_____ in thee._____

written for the M.M.A. in memory of Stanley Milne

How like an angel came I down

Thomas Traherne (1636-74)   Malcolm Archer (b. 1952)

how their glo-ry did me crown! The world re-sem-bled his e-

-ter-ni-ty, in which my soul did walk;_____ And

-ter-ni-ty, in which my soul did walk;_____

ev-'ry-thing that I did see_____ did with me

And ev-'ry-thing____ that I did see_____ did with me

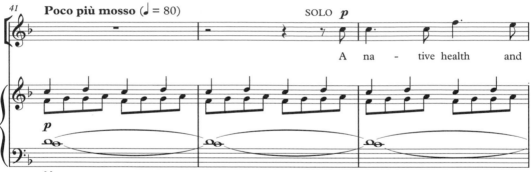

A na - tive health and

Man.

in - no - cence with - in my bones did grow, and

while my God did all his glo - ries show, I felt a

Ped.

vi - gour in my sense that was all spi - rit;

How lovely are Thy dwellings fair

Paraphrase of Psalm 84
by John Milton (1608-74)

Eric H. Thiman (1900-75)

so near. My soul doth long and
so near. My soul doth long and

al-most die, Thy courts, O Lord, to see: My heart and
al-most die, Thy courts, O Lord, to see: My heart and

flesh a-loud do cry, O liv-ing God, for
flesh a-loud do cry, O liv-ing God, for

Thee._____

Thee._____ Hap - py who in Thy

Hap - py whose strength in Thee doth bide,_____

house re-side, Where Thee they e-ver praise!

poco più mosso

_____ And in their hearts Thy ways! They jour-ney on from

They jour-ney on from

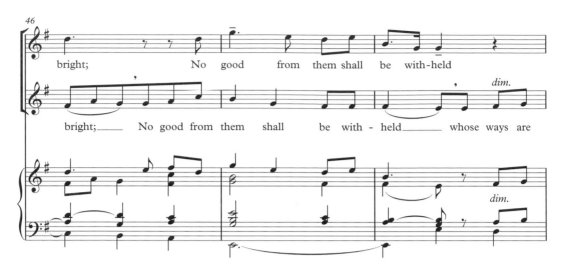

for Richard Halsey and the boys of St Barnabas, Purley

A Hymn to the Virgin

15th century

Robert Spearing (b. 1950)

† If no trumpet is available, this should be played by the organ on a distinctive Solo stop (not necessarily Trumpet).

60

chose for her Son. In quiet he drew To where she was. As the

poco rall.

breve

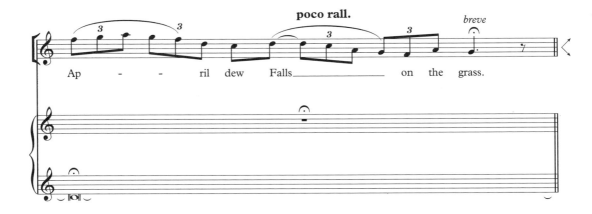

Ap - - ril dew Falls on the grass.

Un poco più mosso

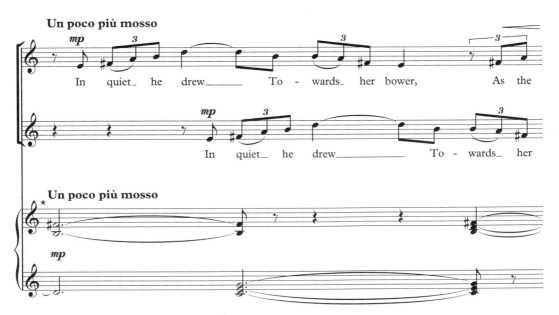

In quiet he drew Towards her bower, As the

In quiet he drew Towards her

* R.H. on a different manual

Both mo-ther and mai-den Was none_ but she: Well may such a

la-dy God's mo-ther be. Al-le-lu — — ia,_

Tempo giusto (♩. = c.56)

Al-le-lu — — ia,_ Al-le-lu-ia,

Al-le-lu-ia, Al-le-lu — — ia,_

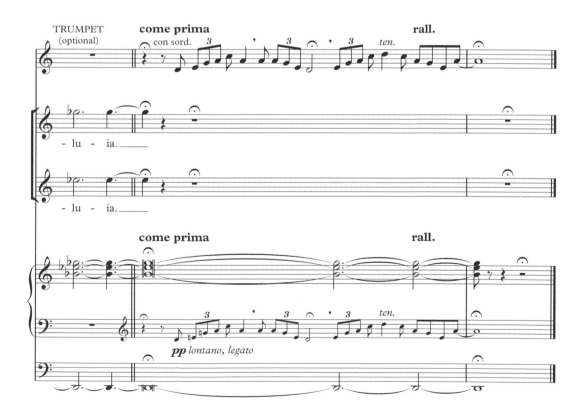

Lift thine eyes

from *Elijah*

Julius Schubring (1806-89)
tr. William Bartholomew (1793-1867)

Felix Mendelssohn (1809-47)

for Arthur Milner

I sing of a maiden

15th century

Bryan Hesford (1930-96)

a) matchless   b) chose   c) falleth

★ optional part

lay,___ As___ dew___ in Ap - ril that fall'th on the spray.

lay, As dew___ in Ap - ril that___ fall'th on the spray.

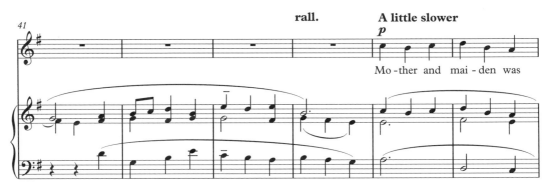

rall. **A little slower**

Mo - ther and mai - den was

ne - ver none but she; Well may such a la - dy God-ès mo - ther

rall.

pp **a tempo** **rall.**

be.

The Lord is my Shepherd
D.706

Psalm 23

Franz Schubert (1797-1828)

The original version for SSAA is also available (NOV 290103)

Thou pre - par - est__ here a ta - ble for me in
Du richt - est__ mir ein Freu - den - mahl im

Thou pre - par - est__ here
Du richt - est__ mir

pre - sence__ of mine e - ne - mies; my head with__ oil Thou a -
An - ge - sicht der Fein - de__ zu, du salbst mein Haupt mit__

a ta - ble for me; my head with__ oil Thou a -
ein Freu - den - mahl, du salbst mein Haupt mit__

-noint - est; my cup__ run-neth o - ver,__ run - neth, run - neth
Ö - le, und schenkst mir__ vol - le,__ vol - le__ Be - cher

-noint - est; my__ cup run-neth o - ver, run - neth, run - neth__
Ö - le, und__ schenkst mir vol - le, vol - le Be - cher__

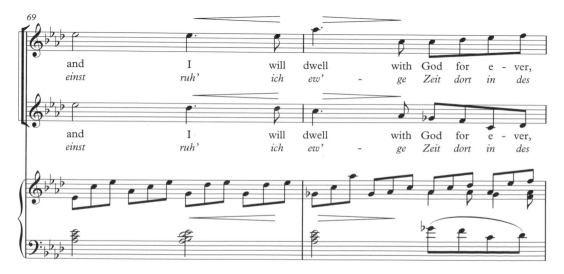

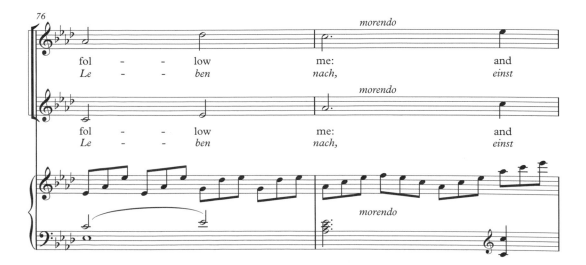

for Douglas Major and the Choir of Washington National Cathedral

Magnificat and Nunc Dimittis
"Washington"

Canticle of Mary
St. Luke, ch.1, vv.46-55

David Hogan (1949-96)

Magnificat

His hand - maid - en._____ For be -

- hold, from hence - forth,___ all ge - ne - ra - tions___ shall call me

bless - ed.

rall.

mer - cy is on them that fear Him____ through - out all

a tempo

mf

ge - ne - ra - tions.____

senza rall.

He hath shown strength with His arm;

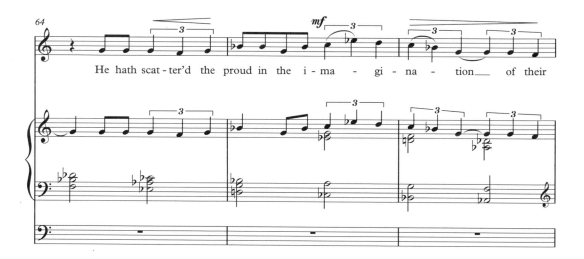

He hath scat-ter'd the proud in the i - ma - gi - na - tion___ of their

hearts.___

He hath put

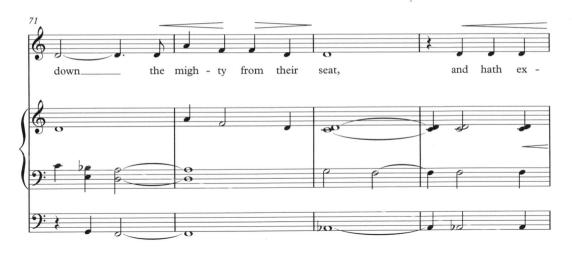

down ___ the migh - ty from their seat, and hath ex -

-alt - - - - ed the hum - ble and meek. ___

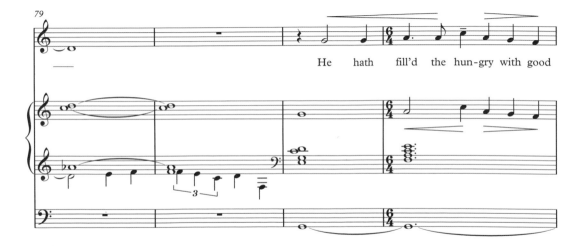

He hath fill'd the hun-gry with good

things; and the rich_____ He hath sent emp - ty a -

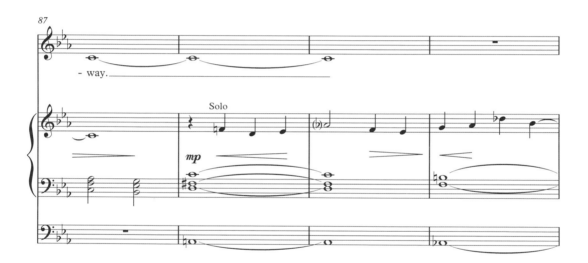

- way._____

Solo

mp

mf

He re - mem-b'ring His mer-cy hath hol-pen His ser-vant

Is - ra - el; as He pro-mised to our fore - fa - thers, A - bra - ham

poco rall. Tempo I

and His seed for e - ver.

Glo - ry be to the Fa - ther

and to the Son, and to the Ho - ly Ghost;___

As it was in the be -

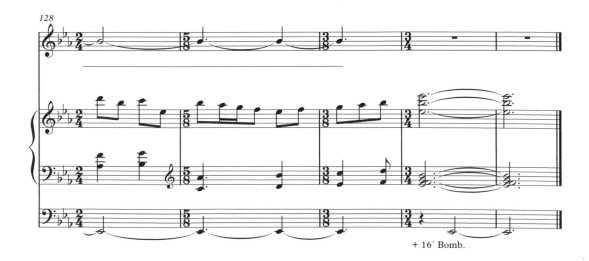

Nunc Dimittis

Prayer of Simeon
St. Luke, ch.2, vv.29-32

Lord ___ now let - test thou Thy ser - vant ___ de - part ___ in peace, ___ ac - cord - ing to Thy word. ___ For ___

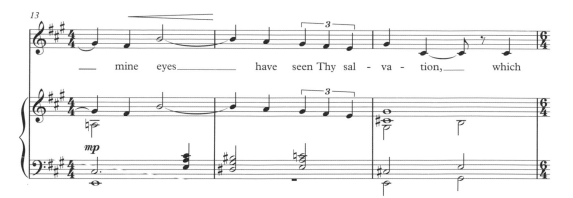

mine eyes_____ have seen Thy sal - va - tion,_____ which

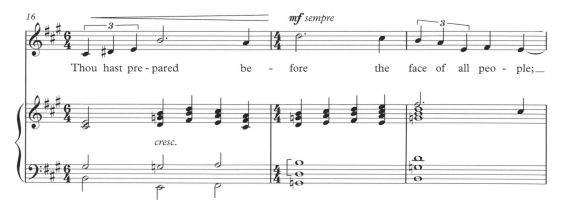

Thou hast pre - pared be - fore the face of all peo - ple;_____

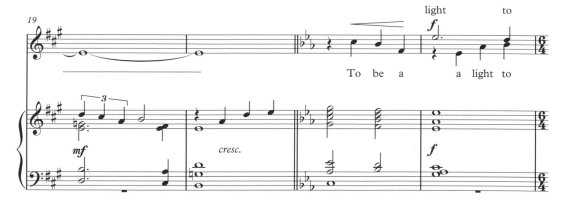

To be a a light to

light-en the Gen-tiles, and to be the glo - ry

Man.

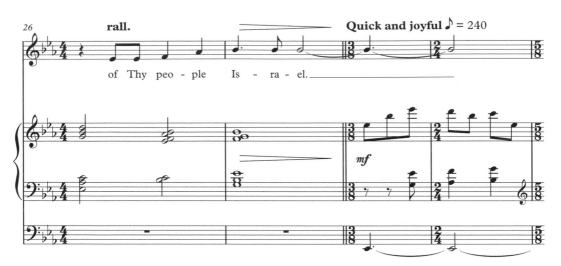

of Thy peo - ple Is - ra - el.

Glo - ry be to the Fa - ther

and to the Son, and to the Ho - ly Ghost;____

As it

was in the be - gin - ning, is now and e - ver shall be,____

world with - out end. A - men,

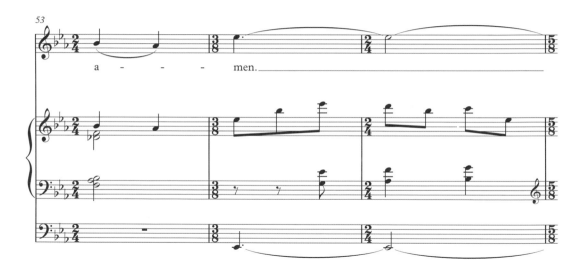

a - - - men.

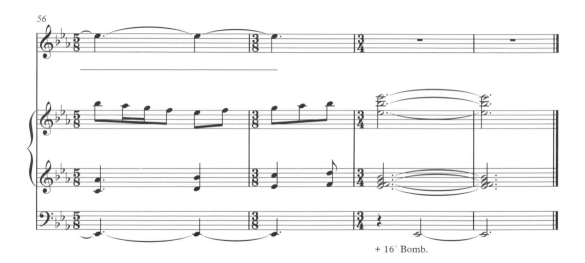

+ 16′ Bomb.

A New Year Carol

Text: anon.

Robert Ruutel (b. 1964)

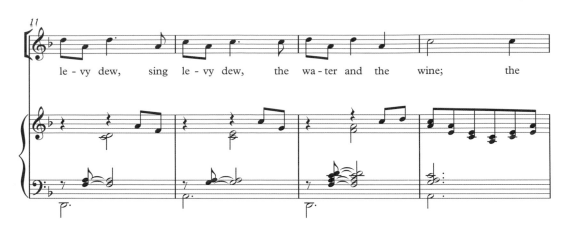

le - vy dew, sing le - vy dew, the wa - ter and the wine; the

se - ven bright gold wires and the bu - gles that do shine.

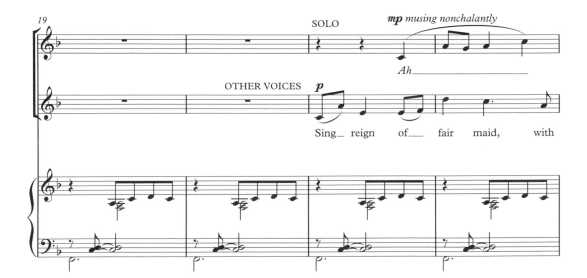

SOLO

mp musing nonchalantly

Ah

OTHER VOICES *p*

Sing reign of fair maid, with

mm_____ ah_____ ah_____ mm_____

gold up - on her toe, o - pen you the West Door and

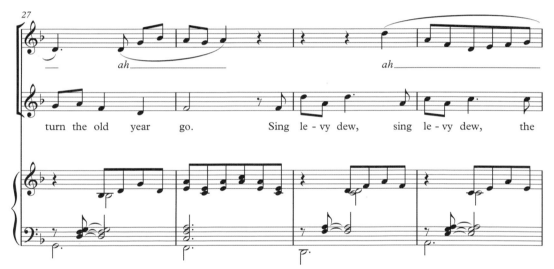

___ ah_____ ah_____

turn the old year go. Sing le - vy dew, sing le - vy dew, the

___ mm_____ ah_____ mm_____

wa - ter and the wine; the se - ven bright gold wires and the

ah_____

bu - gles that do shine.

Flute

TUTTI

Sing_ reign of__ fair maid with gold up - on her chin,

o - pen you the East Door and let the New Year in. Sing

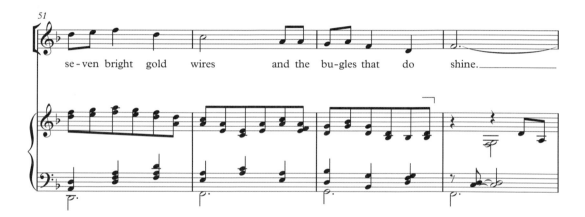

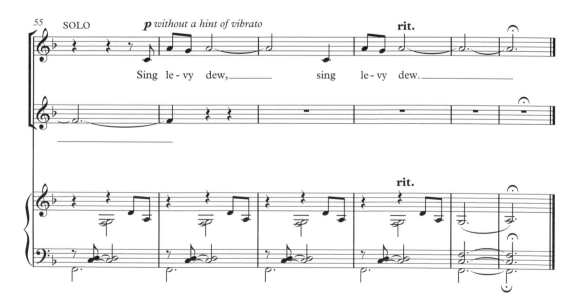

le - vy dew, sing le - vy dew, the wa - ter and the wine; the

se - ven bright gold wires and the bu - gles that do shine.

SOLO **p** *without a hint of vibrato* **rit.**

Sing le - vy dew, sing le - vy dew.

Wells, Midnight 21st January MMI

for the baptism of Sofia
and for Les Petits Chanteurs de Saint-André de Colmar

Notre Père

St. Matthew, ch.6, vv.9-13

John Tavener (b.1944)

* ♯ denotes a microtone, a characteristic "break in the voice" of Byzantine chant.

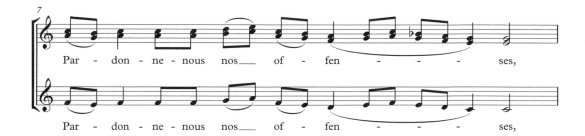

Par - don - ne - nous nos__ of - fen - - - ses,

Par - don - ne - nous nos__ of - fen - - - ses,

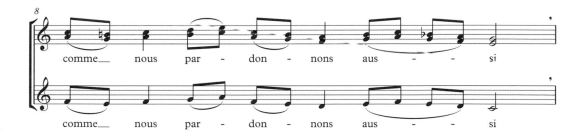

comme__ nous par - don - nons aus - - si

comme__ nous par - don - nons aus - - si

à ceux__ qui__ nous ont__ of - - fen - sés,

à ceux__ qui__ nous ont__ of - - fen - sés,

et ne nous__ sou - mets pas à la ten - ta - ti - on,

et ne nous__ sou - mets pas à la ten - ta - ti - on,

rit. - - - - - molto - - - - - - a tempo

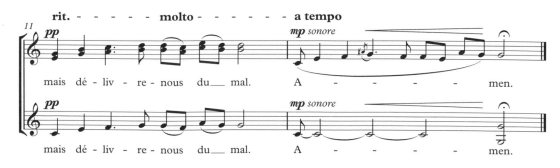

mais dé - liv - re - nous du__ mal. A - - - - men.

mais dé - liv - re - nous du__ mal. A - - - - men.

Naldretts
Sunday of the Blind Man 1996

Nunc Dimittis

St. Luke, ch.2, vv.29-32

Geoffrey Burgon (b. 1941)

Lord, now let-test Thou thy ser - vant de-part in peace,___ ac - cord-ing to___ thy word:___ For mine eyes___ have_ seen

An unaccompanied version for SS soli and SATB chorus is also available

Panis angelicus

St. Thomas Aquinas (1225-74)

César Franck (1822-90)
arr. Henry Geehl (1881-1961)

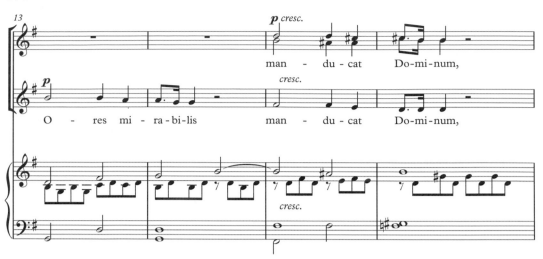

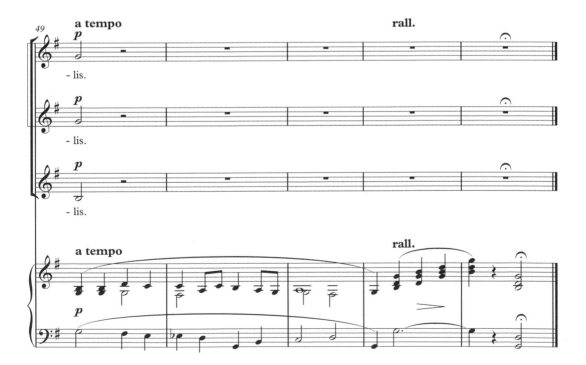

May the Bread of Angels be bread for mankind,
Give an end to symbols in this heavenly bread:
What a marvel! A poor, humble slave
Receives the Lord.

Pie Jesu

from the Sequence at the
Mass for the Dead

Andrew Lloyd Webber (b. 1948)
(Arranged, by permission, for *High Praise 2*)

Original version (Soprano/Treble Soloists and SATB Chorus) available (RUG 37326)

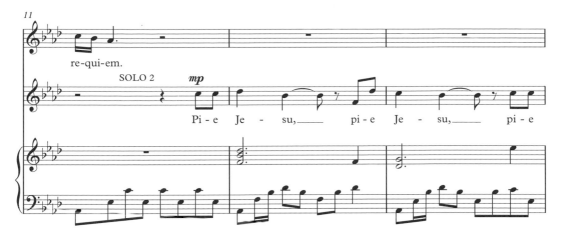

Praise

George Herbert (1593-1633)

George Dyson (1883-1964)

Let all the world in ev-'ry cor-ner sing my God and King. The heav'ns are not too high, His praise may thi-ther fly, The earth is not too low, His prais-

for Morwenna

A prayer

Irene Cavenaugh

Richard Lloyd (b. 1933)

-dore and be all Thine.___

Sw.

cresc.

TUTTI *mf*

Lord, I would give this all of

mf

Man.

me If I might live a - while in Thee: If more and

more this heart of mine Might Thee___ a - dore and be all

cresc.

cresc.

Ped.

Thine. Wilt Thou then take a gift so

Thine. Wilt Thou then take a gift so small

small That for Thy sake is none___ at all?

That for Thy sake is none at all?___ E'en such as

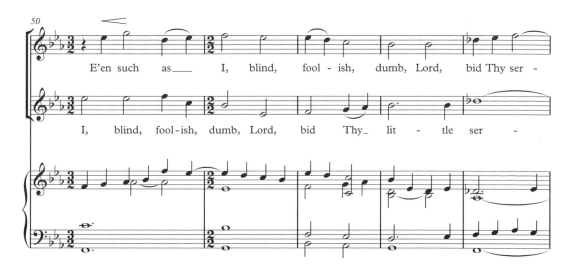

E'en such as___ I, blind, fool - ish, dumb, Lord, bid Thy ser -

I, blind, fool-ish, dumb, Lord, bid Thy_ lit - tle ser -

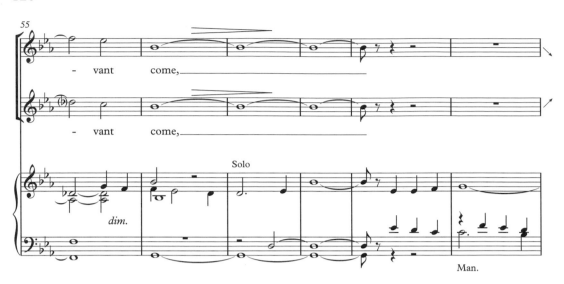

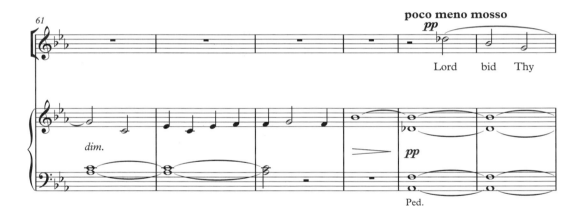

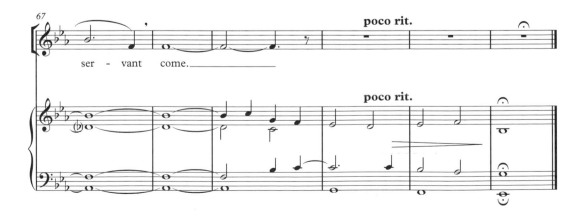

In Memoriam – Sheila Mossman

Prayer of St. Francis of Assisi

Arthur Bliss (1891-1975)

faith. Where there is des - pair, hope.

Where there is dark - ness, light.

Where there is sad - ness, joy, joy, joy.

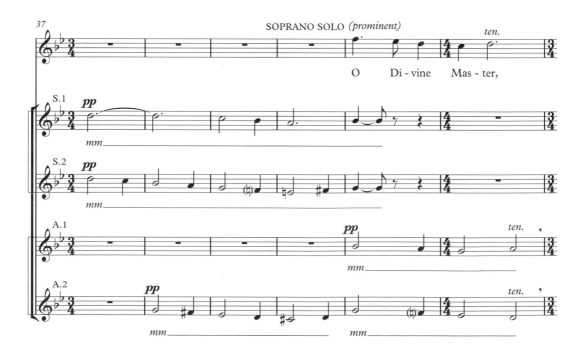

SOPRANO SOLO *(prominent)*

O Di - vine Mas - ter,

S.1 *pp*

mm

S.2 *pp*

mm

A.1 *pp*

mm

A.2 *pp*

mm mm

slightly quicker ♩ = c.80
(very distinct words)

for it is in giv - ing that we re - ceive,

it is in par - don - ing that we are par - doned, and

that it is in dy - ing that we are born to E -

rall. *ten.* **slightly slower**

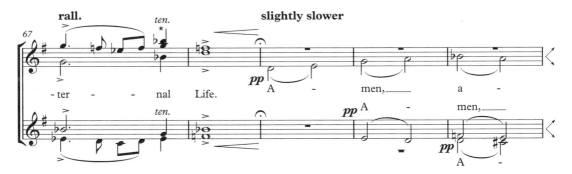

-ter - nal Life. A - men, a - men, a -

poco rall.

A - men, a - men, a - men, a - men.
-men, a - men, a - men, a - men, a - men.
a - men, a - men, a - men, a - men.
-men, a - men, a - men, a - men.

* high B flat optional for a few voices

for Charlotte Frye and the Choristers of Saint Paul's Church, Fairfield

The Preces and Responses

The Invitatory

John Abdenour (b. 1962)

VOICES

And our mouth— shall shew forth———— thy praise.

SOLO
(Precentor)*

O Lord, open thou our lips,

ORGAN

O Lord, make haste to help us.

O———————— make haste to— help us.

O God, make speed to save us.

Man.

* May be sung by a soprano an octave higher.

126

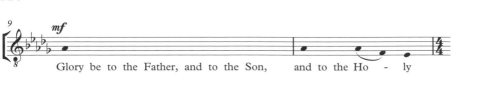

Glory be to the Father, and to the Son, and to the Ho - ly

and e - ver shall be:
is now,
As it was in the be - gin - ning,
Ghost:

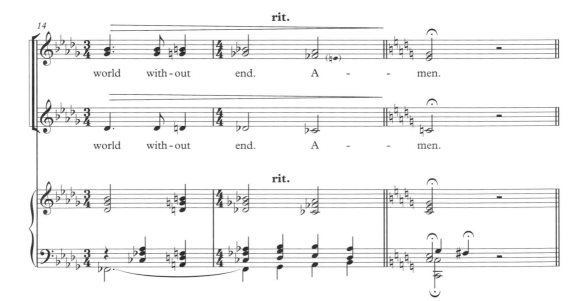

world with-out end. A - men.
world with-out end. A - men.

The Prayers

If the *Kyrie* is omitted, the Lord's Prayer follows immediately.

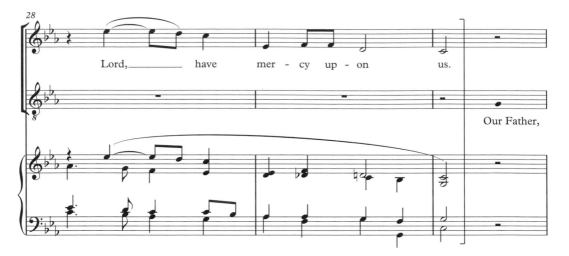

Lord,———— have mer - cy up - on us.

Our Father,

who art in . . . deliver us from evil. [For thine . . . ever and ever.] A - men.

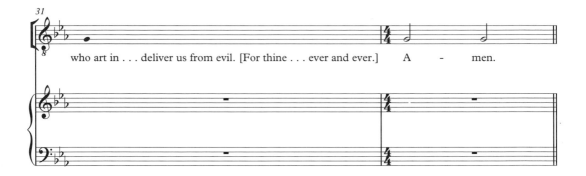

The Suffrages

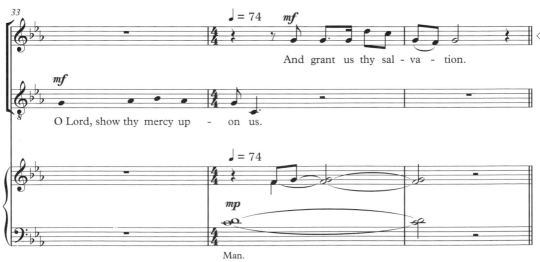

And grant us thy sal - va - tion.

O Lord, show thy mercy up - on us.

Man.

fight - eth for us but on - ly thou, O God.

Man.

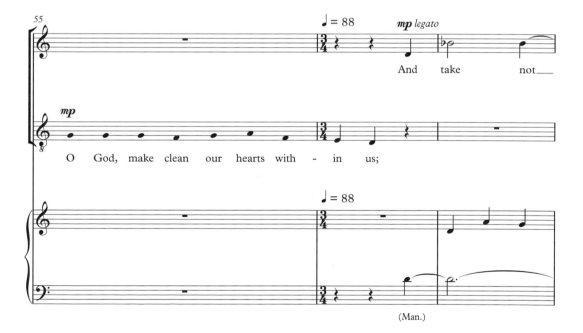

♩ = 88   *mp* *legato*

And take not

O God, make clean our hearts with - in us;

♩ = 88

(Man.)

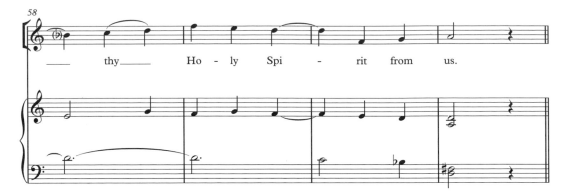

thy___ Ho - ly Spi - rit from us.

The Collects

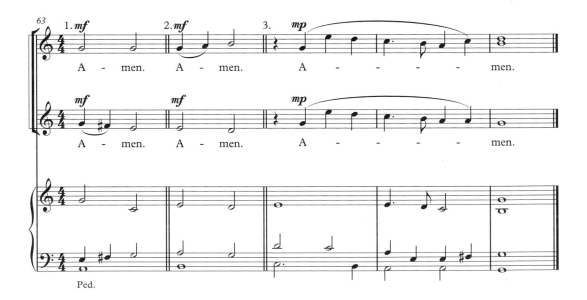

A - men. A - men. A - - - - men.

A - men. A - men. A - - - - men.

Ped.

for Vincent Edwards and the St. Bartholomew's Choristers
for the sixth Annual Choir Festival, New York City, June 2002

Psalm 150

Barry Rose (b. 1934)

praise him, in the fir - ma - ment of__ his__ power.

Praise him, in his

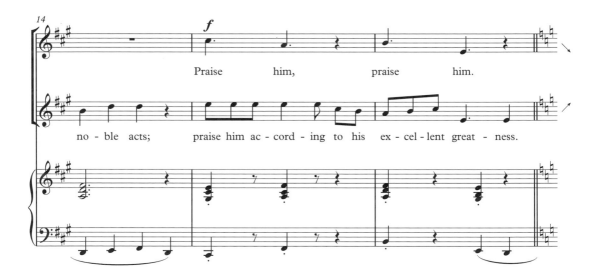

Praise him, praise him.

no - ble acts; praise him ac - cord - ing to his ex - cel - lent great - ness.

Praise him with the sound of the trum-pet;

Solo reed

praise him up-on the lute and harp. Praise him in the cym - bals,

cym - bals, cym - bals, dan - ces,_ Praise him on the strings_ and_

pipe. Praise him up-on the well-tuned cym-bals, Praise him, on the

lóud cym-bals! Let ev-'ry-thing that hath breath,_ let ev-'ry-thing that hath

* lower part ossia A♭, if easier to sing

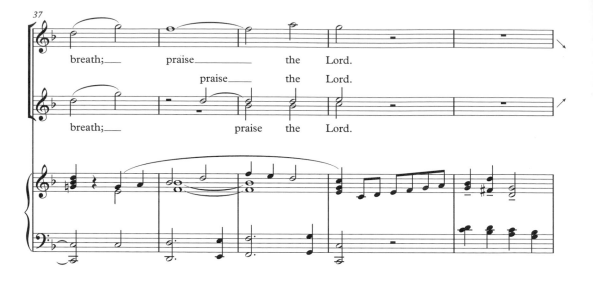

breath;___ praise___ the Lord.

praise___ the Lord.

breath;___ praise the Lord.

TUTTI

f

Glo - ry be to the Fa - ther, and to the Son and

to the Ho - ly Ghost, as it was in the be - gin - ning is

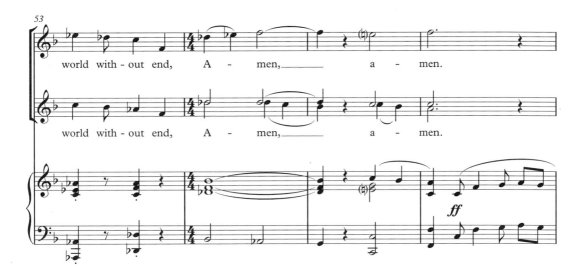

Somerset, April 2002

for Barry Rose and the Choristers of St. Albans Cathedral

Through the day

Thomas Kelly (1769-1854)

Alan Ridout (1934-96)

SOPRANO: Through the day thy love has spared us;

Now we lay us down to rest;_____ Through the si - lent

ALTO: Through the si - lent

Man.

watch - es guard us, Let no foe our peace mo - lest;

watch - es guard us, Let no foe our peace mo - lest;

Je - sus, thou our guar - di-an be; Sweet it is to trust in thee.

Je - sus, thou our guar - di-an be; Sweet it is to trust in thee.

The virgin's slumber-song

(Mariä Wiegenlied)

Martin Boelitz (1874-1918)
tr. Edward Teschemacher

Max Reger (1873-1916)
Op.76, No.52

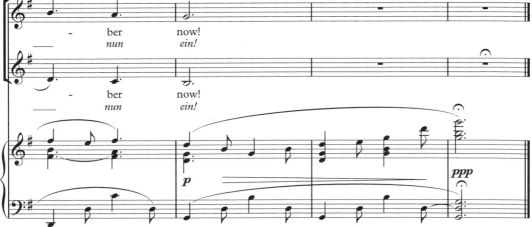

Who can express the noble acts of the Lord?

from *O give thanks unto the Lord*

Psalm 106, v.2; Psalm 86, vv.5, 9-10   Samuel Sebastian Wesley (1810-76)

good_ and gra - cious un - to all them____ that call on

Thee, on all__ that_ call_ on_ Thee, of great_

mer - cy un - to all__ them, all them that call, that call up -

- on Thee.

All na-tions whom Thou hast made shall come and

wor-ship Thee, O Lord, and shall glo-ri-

-fy Thy Name,_____ shall glo-ri-fy Thy

Name. For Thou art good and do-est won - - drous

things: for on-ly Thou art ho-ly, Thou on-ly art the Lord.__ For

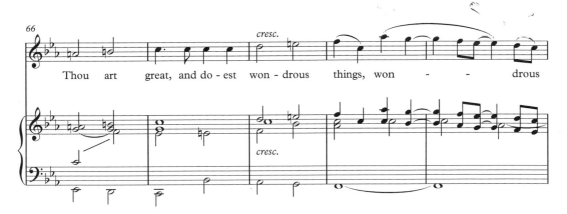

Thou art great, and do-est won-drous things, won - - - drous

things, won - - - - - - drous things.

Who can ex-press, who can ex-press the no-ble, no-ble acts of the

Lord, or shew forth all His praise? or shew forth

all His praise, all, all His praise? or shew forth all

His praise, shew forth all His

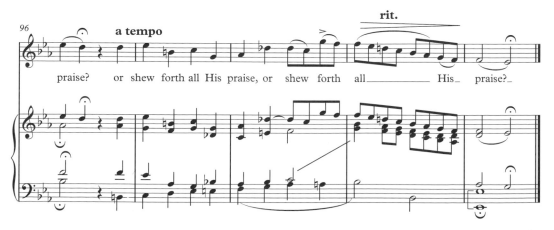

praise? or shew forth all His praise, or shew forth all His praise?